VEGETARIAN DIABETIC DIET COOKBOOK FOR NEWLY DIAGNOSED

Quick and Delicious 30-Day plant-based
Recipes to manage Pre-diabetes and Reverse
Type-2 diabetes with 30-Day Meal Plan

By

Dr. Mary D. Torres

TABLE OF CONTENTS

INTRODUCTION

My uncle Mike, who was once faced with the challenge of managing type 2 diabetes. He felt overwhelmed by the diagnosis and uncertain about the path ahead. But Mike chose to view his diagnosis as an opportunity for positive change. He decided to explore the potential of a vegetarian diet in his diabetes management journey.

As Mike transitioned to a vegetarian lifestyle, he discovered a world of delicious and nourishing foods that supported his health goals. He became aware of the incredible variety of plant-based ingredients that not only satisfied his taste buds but also helped regulate his blood sugar levels. Through careful planning and a deep understanding of nutrition, Mike learned how to create balanced and flavorful meals that worked in harmony with his body's needs.

In time, Mike's efforts paid off. With the guidance of healthcare professionals and the support of resources like this cookbook, he found himself experiencing improved energy levels, better weight management, and more stable blood sugar levels. Mike's story is a testament to the transformative potential of combining vegetarian nutrition with diabetes management.

CHAPTER 1
Understanding Type 2 Diabetes

What is Type 2 Diabetes? Type 2 diabetes is a chronic metabolic disorder that affects how your body uses insulin, a hormone responsible for regulating blood sugar (glucose) levels. Insulin helps cells absorb glucose from the bloodstream to use as energy. In type 2 diabetes, your body either doesn't produce enough insulin or becomes resistant to its effects, leading to elevated blood sugar levels.

This condition develops over time and is often associated with lifestyle factors such as obesity, physical inactivity, and poor dietary habits. It is more common in adults, but it can also occur in children and adolescents.

Key Characteristics of Type 2 Diabetes:

Insulin Resistance: Cells become less responsive to the effects of insulin, resulting in higher blood sugar levels. The body compensates by producing more insulin, leading to higher levels of both insulin and glucose in the bloodstream.

Beta Cell Dysfunction: Over time, the insulin-producing cells in the pancreas (beta cells) may become impaired, leading to decreased insulin production.

Hyperglycemia: Elevated blood sugar levels (hyperglycemia) are a hallmark of type 2 diabetes. This can lead to various symptoms and complications if not managed properly.

Symptoms: Common symptoms include increased thirst, frequent urination, unexplained weight loss, fatigue, blurred vision, and slow-healing wounds.

Risk Factors: Factors that increase the risk of developing type 2 diabetes include obesity, sedentary lifestyle, family history, age (particularly over 45), and certain ethnic backgrounds.

Complications: If not well managed, type 2 diabetes can lead to various complications such as cardiovascular disease, kidney disease, nerve damage (neuropathy), eye problems (retinopathy), and foot problems.

Causes and Symptoms

Type 2 diabetes is a complex condition influenced by both genetic and lifestyle factors. While the exact causes aren't fully understood, several key factors contribute to its development:

Insulin Resistance: Cells become resistant to the effects of insulin, making it harder for glucose to enter the cells and be used for energy.

Genetics: Family history of diabetes can increase your risk. Certain genetic traits can make you more susceptible to insulin resistance and diabetes.

Obesity: Excess body weight, especially around the abdomen, is a significant risk factor for type 2 diabetes. Fat tissue, particularly visceral fat, contributes to insulin resistance.

Physical Inactivity: Sedentary lifestyles reduce insulin sensitivity and increase the risk of diabetes. Regular physical activity helps maintain healthy blood sugar levels.

Unhealthy Diet: Diets high in processed foods, sugary beverages, and refined carbohydrates contribute to weight gain and insulin resistance.

Age: Risk increases with age, particularly after 45, due to factors like reduced muscle mass and physical activity.

Ethnic Background: Certain ethnic groups, such as African Americans, Hispanic Americans, Native Americans, and Asian Americans, are at higher risk.

Gestational Diabetes: Women who had gestational diabetes during pregnancy are at a higher risk of developing type 2 diabetes later in life.

Symptoms of Type 2 Diabetes:

Type 2 diabetes can develop gradually, and some people may not experience noticeable symptoms initially. Common symptoms include:

Increased Thirst and Urination: Excess glucose in the bloodstream leads to increased thirst and frequent urination.

Unexplained Weight Loss: Despite eating more, unexplained weight loss may occur due to the body's inability to use glucose for energy.

Fatigue: Cells don't receive enough glucose for energy, leading to fatigue and weakness.

Blurred Vision: High blood sugar levels can affect the lenses of the eyes, causing blurry vision.

Slow Healing: Wounds and infections take longer to heal due to compromised circulation and immune function.

Tingling or Numbness: Nerve damage (neuropathy) can cause tingling, numbness, or pain in the hands and feet.

Recurrent Infections: High blood sugar weakens the immune system, making you more susceptible to infections.

Darkened Skin: A condition called acanthosis nigricans can cause dark, thickened patches of skin, often around the neck or armpits.

Nutritional Guidelines for Diabetics

Proper nutrition plays a crucial role in managing type 2 diabetes. A well-balanced diet can help regulate blood sugar levels, improve insulin sensitivity, and reduce the risk of complications. Below is some nutritional guideline to consider.

Carbohydrate Management:

- Focus on complex carbohydrates such as whole grains (brown rice, quinoa, whole wheat), legumes, and vegetables.
- Monitor portion sizes to control carbohydrate intake and prevent spikes in blood sugar levels.
- Choose high-fiber foods to slow down the absorption of glucose and promote satiety.

Balanced Meals:

- Create balanced meals that include lean proteins (poultry, fish, tofu, legumes), healthy fats (nuts, seeds, avocados, olive oil), and non-starchy vegetables.
- Incorporate protein and healthy fats to help stabilize blood sugar levels and keep you feeling full.

Fruits and Vegetables:

- Choose a variety of colorful fruits and vegetables rich in vitamins, minerals, and fiber.
- Be mindful of portion sizes for fruits, as they contain natural sugars.

Sugar and Sweeteners:

Limit added sugars and sugary foods such as candies, pastries, and sugary beverages.

Opt for natural sweeteners like stevia or small amounts of honey or maple syrup if needed.

Glycemic Index (GI):

Learn about the glycemic index of foods, which indicates how quickly they raise blood sugar levels.

Favor low-GI foods to help manage blood sugar spikes.

Portion Control:

- Pay attention to portion sizes to prevent overeating and manage calorie intake.
- Use smaller plates and bowls to help control portion sizes visually.

Healthy Cooking Methods:

- Choose cooking methods that require less added fat, such as grilling, baking, steaming, and sautéing with minimal oil.
- Avoid deep-frying and excessive use of butter or oils.

Regular Meals and Snacks:

- Eat regular meals and snacks spaced throughout the day to maintain stable blood sugar levels.
- Avoid skipping meals, as this can lead to blood sugar fluctuations.

Hydration:

- Stay hydrated by drinking plenty of water throughout the day.
- Limit sugary beverages and opt for water, herbal tea, or unsweetened drinks.

Limit Processed Foods:

Minimize intake of highly processed and refined foods, which often contain hidden sugars and unhealthy fats.

CHAPTER 2
The Vegetarian Lifestyle

Who is a Vegan? A vegetarian is an individual who follows a dietary pattern that excludes meat, which includes animal flesh such as poultry, red meat, and seafood.

Types of Vegetarian Diets

1. Lacto-Vegetarian:

Excludes: Meat, poultry, seafood, and eggs.

Includes: Dairy products such as milk, cheese, yogurt, and butter.

2. Ovo-Vegetarian:

Excludes: Meat, poultry, seafood, and dairy products.

Includes: Eggs and egg products.

3. Lacto-Ovo-Vegetarian:

Excludes: Meat, poultry, and seafood.

Includes: Both dairy products and eggs.

4. Vegan:

Excludes: All animal products, including meat, poultry, seafood, dairy products, eggs, and ingredients derived from animals like honey and gelatin.

Embraces: Plant-based foods like vegetables, fruits, legumes, grains, nuts, seeds, and plant-derived alternatives.

5. Pescatarian:

Excludes: Meat and poultry.

Includes: Seafood, along with plant-based foods and sometimes dairy and eggs.

6. Flexitarian or Semi-Vegetarian:

Practiced by individuals who primarily follow a plant-based diet but occasionally include small amounts of meat, poultry, or seafood.

7. Raw Food Vegetarian:

Involves consuming only raw, unprocessed plant-based foods, avoiding cooking and animal products.

Benefits of A Vegetarian Diet for Diabetes Management

Adopting a well-balanced vegetarian diet can offer a range of benefits for individuals with type 2 diabetes. By focusing on nutrient-rich plant-based foods, you can improve blood sugar control, enhance insulin sensitivity, and reduce the risk of complications. These are some key advantages of a vegetarian diet for diabetes management:

Improved Blood Sugar Control:

Plant-based diets are often rich in fiber, which slows down the digestion and absorption of carbohydrates, leading to steadier blood sugar levels.

Complex carbohydrates found in whole grains, legumes, and vegetables have a lower glycemic index, reducing the risk of blood sugar spikes.

Weight Management:

Vegetarian diets, when centered around whole foods and controlled portions, can aid in weight loss or weight management.

Weight loss improves insulin sensitivity and can lead to better blood sugar control.

Heart Health:

A vegetarian diet is naturally lower in saturated fat and cholesterol compared to diets that include meat.

Reduced intake of saturated fats supports heart health and lowers the risk of cardiovascular complications often associated with diabetes.

Healthy Fats:

Plant-based diets emphasize healthy fats such as those found in nuts, seeds, avocados, and olive oil.

These fats support overall health and can help manage cholesterol levels.

Rich in Fiber:

Vegetarian diets are abundant in dietary fiber, which aids digestion, promotes satiety, and helps regulate blood sugar levels.

Fiber also supports gut health and contributes to a feeling of fullness.

Nutrient Density:

Plant-based foods offer a diverse array of vitamins, minerals, and antioxidants that support overall well-being.

A varied diet provides essential nutrients that contribute to immune function, bone health, and more.

Reduced Risk of Complications:

A well-managed vegetarian diet can help reduce the risk of diabetes-related complications, such as cardiovascular disease, kidney problems, and nerve damage.

Lower Blood Pressure:

The inclusion of whole foods in a vegetarian diet can lead to lower blood pressure levels, benefiting heart health.

Satiety and Satisfaction:

Protein-rich plant foods and fiber contribute to a feeling of fullness and satisfaction after meals.

This can help prevent overeating and promote weight management.

Environmental Impact:

Plant-based diets tend to have a lower environmental footprint, contributing to sustainability efforts.

Reducing meat consumption can decrease greenhouse gas emissions and conserve resources.

CHAPTER 3
BREAKFAST RECIPES

1. Veggie Omelette:

Ingredients:

2 eggs or 4 egg whites

1/4 cup chopped bell peppers; 1/4 cup chopped onions

1/2 cup chopped spinach, Salt and pepper to taste

2 tablespoons low-fat cheese (optional)

Instructions:

Whisk eggs or egg whites in a bowl and season with salt and pepper.

Heat a non-stick pan over medium heat and lightly coat with cooking spray.

Add bell peppers and onions, sauté for a few minutes until softened.

Add spinach and cook until wilted.

Pour the egg mixture into the pan and let it cook until set.

Sprinkle cheese on one half of the omelette and fold it over.

Cook for another minute until the cheese melts.

Slide the omelette onto a plate and serve.

2. Greek Yogurt Parfait:

Ingredients:

1/2 cup non-fat Greek yogurt

1/4 cup mixed berries (blueberries, raspberries, strawberries)

1 teaspoon honey or a sprinkle of cinnamon

1 tablespoon chopped nuts (e.g., almonds, walnuts)

Instructions:

In a glass or bowl, layer Greek yogurt, mixed berries, and honey or cinnamon.

Top with chopped nuts.

Enjoy immediately.

3. Overnight Chia Pudding:

Ingredients:

2 tablespoons chia seeds

1/2 cup unsweetened almond milk

1/4 teaspoon vanilla extract

1/4 cup mixed berries

1 tablespoon sliced almonds

Instructions:

In a bowl, mix chia seeds, almond milk, and vanilla extract.

Cover and refrigerate overnight.

In the morning, stir the chia pudding and top with mixed berries and sliced almonds.

Serve cold.

4. Whole Grain Toast with Avocado:

Ingredients:

1 slice whole grain bread, toasted

1/4 ripe avocado, mashed

2-3 slices tomato

Pinch of black pepper

Instructions:

Spread mashed avocado on the toasted bread.

Top with tomato slices and a sprinkle of black pepper.

Enjoy as an open-faced sandwich.

5. *Quinoa Breakfast Bowl:*

Ingredients:

1/2 cup cooked quinoa

2 tablespoons chopped almonds

1/2 small apple, diced

1/4 cup unsweetened almond milk

Instructions:

In a bowl, combine cooked quinoa, chopped almonds, diced apple, and almond milk.

Mix well and serve.

6. *Smoothie Bowl:*

Ingredients:

1/2 cup frozen mixed berries

1 small banana, 1 cup spinach or kale

1 scoop plant-based protein powder

1/2 cup unsweetened almond milk

Sliced banana, chia seeds, chopped nuts for topping

Instructions:

Blend frozen berries, banana, spinach or kale, protein powder, and almond milk until smooth.

Pour the smoothie into a bowl.

Top with sliced banana, chia seeds, and chopped nuts.

7. *Vegetable Scramble:*

Ingredients:

1/2 cup diced zucchini

1/4 cup diced bell peppers

1/4 cup diced onions

1/2 cup diced tomatoes

1/2 cup scrambled tofu or 2 eggs, beaten

Salt and pepper to taste

Cooking spray

Instructions:

Heat a non-stick pan over medium heat and coat with cooking spray.

Add diced zucchini, bell peppers, and onions. Sauté until softened.

Add diced tomatoes and cook for a minute.

Push the veggies to the side and add scrambled tofu or beaten eggs to the pan.

Cook, stirring occasionally, until eggs are set or tofu is heated through.

Season with salt and pepper.

Serve warm.

8. Oatmeal with Nut Butter:

Ingredients:

1/2 cup steel-cut oats

1 cup water or unsweetened almond milk

1 tablespoon nut butter (almond, peanut, or your choice)

1 tablespoon sliced almonds

1/4 banana, sliced

Instructions:

In a saucepan, bring oats and water or almond milk to a boil.

Reduce heat and simmer until oats are cooked and the mixture thickens.

Transfer the oatmeal to a bowl and swirl in the nut butter.

Top with sliced almonds and banana slices.

9. *Cottage Cheese Breakfast Bowl:*

Ingredients:

1/2 cup low-fat cottage cheese

1/2 small peach, diced

Pinch of cinnamon

1 tablespoon chopped walnuts

Instructions:

In a bowl, combine cottage cheese, diced peach, and a pinch of cinnamon.

Top with chopped walnuts.

Enjoy as is or with a sprinkle of cinnamon.

10. Breakfast Burrito:

Ingredients:

1 whole wheat tortilla

2 eggs, scrambled

1/4 cup black beans, drained and rinsed

1/4 cup sautéed spinach

2 tablespoons salsa

Instructions:

Warm the whole wheat tortilla.

Fill with scrambled eggs, black beans, sautéed spinach, and salsa.

Roll the tortilla into a burrito.

Serve warm.

11. Berry-Banana Smoothie:
Ingredients:

1/2 cup frozen mixed berries

1 ripe banana, 1/2 cup unsweetened Greek yogurt

1 cup spinach, 1/2 cup water or unsweetened almond milk

Instructions:

Blend frozen berries, banana, Greek yogurt, spinach, and water or almond milk until smooth.

Pour into a glass and enjoy.

11. Almond Butter Toast with Berries:

Ingredients:

1 slice whole grain bread, toasted

1 tablespoon almond butter

1/4 cup sliced strawberries or raspberries

Instructions:

Spread almond butter on the toasted bread.

Top with sliced strawberries or raspberries.

Enjoy as an open-faced sandwich.

12. Veggie Breakfast Wrap:

Ingredients:

1 whole wheat tortilla

2 eggs or scrambled tofu

1/4 cup sautéed mushrooms

1/4 cup sautéed spinach

1/4 cup diced tomatoes

Instructions:

Warm the whole wheat tortilla.

Fill with scrambled eggs or tofu, sautéed mushrooms, spinach, and diced tomatoes.

Roll the tortilla into a wrap.

Serve warm.

14. Apple Cinnamon Oatmeal:

Ingredients:

1/2 cup rolled oats, 1 cup water

1/2 small apple, diced, 1/4 teaspoon cinnamon

1 tablespoon chopped walnuts

Instructions:

In a saucepan, bring oats and water to a boil.

Add diced apple and cinnamon. Simmer until oats are cooked and mixture thickens.

Transfer the oatmeal to a bowl and top with chopped walnuts.

15. Nutty Quinoa Porridge:

Ingredients:

1/2 cup cooked quinoa

1/4 cup unsweetened almond milk

2 tablespoons chopped dried fruits (apricots, raisins)

Pinch of cinnamon

1 tablespoon chopped nuts (e.g., almonds, walnuts)

Instructions:

In a bowl, combine cooked quinoa and almond milk.

Stir in chopped dried fruits and cinnamon.

Top with chopped nuts.

Serve warm.

CHAPTER 4
LUNCH RECIPES

1. Chickpea Salad:

Ingredients:

1 cup cooked chickpeas (canned or boiled)

1/2 cup diced cucumber

1/2 cup diced tomatoes

1/4 cup diced red onion

1/4 cup chopped parsley

2 tablespoons lemon juice

1 tablespoon olive oil

Salt and pepper to taste

Instructions:

In a bowl, combine chickpeas, cucumber, tomatoes, red onion, and parsley.

In a separate bowl, whisk lemon juice, olive oil, salt, and pepper.

Drizzle the dressing over the salad and toss to combine.

Serve chilled.

2. Lentil Soup:

Ingredients:

1 cup dried green or brown lentils, rinsed and drained

1 onion, chopped

2 carrots, diced

2 celery stalks, diced

3 cloves garlic, minced

6 cups vegetable broth

1 teaspoon cumin

1/2 teaspoon turmeric

Salt and pepper to taste

Instructions:

In a large pot, sauté onion, carrots, and celery until softened.

Add garlic, cumin, and turmeric. Cook for another minute.

Add lentils and vegetable broth. Bring to a boil, then reduce heat and simmer until lentils are tender.

Season with salt and pepper.

Serve hot.

3. *Quinoa and Black Bean Bowl:*

Ingredients:

1 cup cooked quinoa

1 cup black beans, drained and rinsed

1/2 cup diced bell peppers (various colors)

1/4 cup chopped red onion

1/4 cup chopped cilantro

Juice of 1 lime

1 tablespoon olive oil

Salt and pepper to taste

Instructions:

In a bowl, combine cooked quinoa, black beans, bell peppers, red onion, and cilantro.

In a separate bowl, whisk lime juice, olive oil, salt, and pepper.

Drizzle the dressing over the quinoa mixture and toss to combine.

Serve at room temperature.

4. Veggie Stir-Fry:

Ingredients:

1 cup mixed vegetables (broccoli, bell peppers, carrots, snap peas)

1/4 cup tofu, cubed

2 tablespoons low-sodium soy sauce

1 teaspoon sesame oil

1/2 teaspoon minced ginger, 1 clove garlic, minced

1 tablespoon chopped green onions

1 teaspoon sesame seeds

Instructions:

Heat sesame oil in a pan over medium-high heat.

Add tofu and cook until golden. Remove from the pan.

In the same pan, sauté mixed vegetables, ginger, and garlic until crisp-tender.

Add cooked tofu back to the pan.

Stir in soy sauce and cook for another minute.

Serve over cooked brown rice or quinoa.

Garnish with chopped green onions and sesame seeds.

5. *Spinach and Feta Stuffed Portobello Mushrooms:*

Ingredients:

2 large Portobello mushrooms, stems removed

1 cup fresh spinach, chopped

1/4 cup crumbled feta cheese

2 tablespoons diced red onion

1 tablespoon olive oil

Salt and pepper to taste

Instructions:

Preheat the oven to 375°F (190°C).

Brush Portobello mushrooms with olive oil and season with salt and pepper.

In a bowl, combine chopped spinach, feta cheese, and red onion.

Stuff the mushrooms with the spinach-feta mixture.

Place mushrooms on a baking sheet and bake for about 15-20 minutes, until mushrooms are tender.

Serve warm.

6. Hummus Wrap:

Ingredients:

1 whole wheat tortilla

1/4 cup hummus

1/2 cup mixed greens

1/4 cup diced cucumbers

1/4 cup diced tomatoes

1/4 cup shredded carrots

2 tablespoons crumbled feta cheese (optional)

Instructions:

Spread hummus on the whole wheat tortilla.

Layer with mixed greens, cucumbers, tomatoes, shredded carrots, and feta cheese.

Roll the tortilla into a wrap.

Serve as is or cut in half.

7. Mediterranean Quinoa Salad:

Ingredients:

1 cup cooked quinoa

1/2 cup diced cucumber

1/2 cup diced tomatoes

1/4 cup diced red onion

1/4 cup chopped Kalamata olives

1/4 cup crumbled feta cheese

2 tablespoons chopped fresh parsley

2 tablespoons lemon juice

1 tablespoon olive oil

Salt and pepper to taste

Instructions:

In a bowl, combine cooked quinoa, cucumber, tomatoes, red onion, olives, feta cheese, and parsley.

In a separate bowl, whisk lemon juice, olive oil, salt, and pepper.

Drizzle the dressing over the quinoa mixture and toss to combine.

Serve chilled.

8. Tofu and Vegetable Stir-Fry:

Ingredients:

1/2 cup cubed tofu

1 cup mixed vegetables (broccoli, bell peppers, carrots)

2 tablespoons low-sodium soy sauce

1 tablespoon hoisin sauce

1/2 teaspoon minced ginger, 1 clove garlic, minced

1 tablespoon chopped green onions

1 teaspoon sesame seeds

Instructions:

Heat a non-stick pan over medium-high heat.

Add tofu and cook until golden. Remove from the pan.

In the same pan, sauté mixed vegetables, ginger, and garlic until crisp-tender.

Add cooked tofu back to the pan.

Stir in soy sauce and hoisin sauce, and cook for another minute.

Serve over cooked brown rice or quinoa.

Garnish with chopped green onions and sesame seeds.

9. *Caprese Salad:*

Ingredients:

1 large tomato, sliced

4-6 fresh mozzarella slices

Fresh basil leaves

1 tablespoon balsamic vinegar reduction

1 tablespoon olive oil

Salt and pepper to taste

Instructions:

Arrange tomato slices and mozzarella slices on a plate, alternating.

Tuck fresh basil leaves between the tomato and mozzarella slices.

Drizzle with balsamic vinegar reduction and olive oil.

Season with salt and pepper.

Serve as a light and refreshing salad.

10. Lentil and Vegetable Stir-Fry:

Ingredients:

1 cup cooked green or brown lentils

1 cup mixed vegetables (bell peppers, carrots, broccoli)

2 tablespoons low-sodium soy sauce

1 teaspoon sesame oil

1/2 teaspoon minced ginger

1 clove garlic, minced

1 tablespoon chopped green onions

1 teaspoon sesame seeds

Instructions:

Heat sesame oil in a pan over medium-high heat.

Add mixed vegetables and sauté until crisp-tender.

Add cooked lentils to the pan.

Stir in soy sauce, ginger, and garlic. Cook for another minute.

Serve over cooked brown rice or quinoa.

Garnish with chopped green onions and sesame seeds.

11. Mediterranean Wrap:

Ingredients:

1 whole wheat tortilla

1/4 cup hummus

1/4 cup diced cucumber

1/4 cup diced tomatoes

1/4 cup diced red onion

1/4 cup chopped Kalamata olives

2 tablespoons crumbled feta cheese

Instructions:

Spread hummus on the whole wheat tortilla.

Layer with cucumber, tomatoes, red onion, Kalamata olives, and feta cheese.

Roll the tortilla into a wrap.

Serve as is or cut in half.

12. *Spinach and Quinoa Stuffed Bell Peppers:*

Ingredients:

2 large bell peppers, halved and seeds removed

1 cup cooked quinoa

1 cup chopped spinach

1/4 cup diced tomatoes

1/4 cup diced red onion

1/4 cup shredded mozzarella cheese

1 tablespoon olive oil

Salt and pepper to taste

Instructions:

Preheat the oven to 375°F (190°C).

Brush bell pepper halves with olive oil and season with salt and pepper.

In a bowl, combine cooked quinoa, chopped spinach, diced tomatoes, red onion, and shredded mozzarella cheese.

Stuff the bell pepper halves with the quinoa-spinach mixture.

Place stuffed bell peppers on a baking sheet and bake for about 20-25 minutes, until peppers are tender.

Serve warm.

13. Black Bean and Corn Salad:

Ingredients:

1 cup black beans, drained and rinsed

1 cup corn kernels (fresh, frozen, or canned)

1/2 cup diced bell peppers (various colors)

1/4 cup diced red onion

1/4 cup chopped cilantro

Juice of 1 lime

1 tablespoon olive oil

Salt and pepper to taste

Instructions:

In a bowl, combine black beans, corn kernels, bell peppers, red onion, and cilantro.

In a separate bowl, whisk lime juice, olive oil, salt, and pepper.

Drizzle the dressing over the salad and toss to combine.

Serve chilled.

14. Roasted Vegetable Wrap:

Ingredients:

1 whole wheat tortilla

1/2 cup roasted mixed vegetables (zucchini, bell peppers, onions)

2 tablespoons hummus

2 tablespoons crumbled goat cheese

Fresh arugula or mixed greens

Instructions:

Spread hummus on the whole wheat tortilla.

Layer with roasted mixed vegetables, crumbled goat cheese, and fresh arugula or mixed greens.

Roll the tortilla into a wrap.

Serve as is or cut in half.

15. *Avocado and Tomato Sandwich:*

Ingredients:

2 slices whole grain bread

1/2 avocado, sliced

1 small tomato, sliced

Handful of arugula or spinach

1 teaspoon lemon juice

Salt and pepper to taste

Instructions:

Toast the slices of whole grain bread.

Layer one slice with avocado slices, tomato slices, and arugula or spinach.

Drizzle with lemon juice and season with salt and pepper.

Top with the other slice of bread to make a sandwich.

Serve as a satisfying sandwich option.

CHAPTER 5
DINNER RECIPES
1. Roasted Vegetable Quinoa Bowl:

Ingredients:

1 cup cooked quinoa

1 cup mixed roasted vegetables (zucchini, bell peppers, carrots, onions)

1/4 cup crumbled feta cheese

2 tablespoons chopped fresh parsley

1 tablespoon balsamic vinegar

1 tablespoon olive oil

Salt and pepper to taste

Instructions:

In a bowl, combine cooked quinoa, mixed roasted vegetables, and feta cheese.

In a separate bowl, whisk balsamic vinegar, olive oil, salt, and pepper.

Drizzle the dressing over the quinoa mixture and toss to combine.

Garnish with chopped parsley.

Serve warm.

2. *Stuffed Bell Peppers with Rice and Beans:*

Ingredients:

4 large bell peppers, halved and seeds removed

1 cup cooked brown rice

1 cup black beans, drained and rinsed

1/2 cup diced tomatoes

1/4 cup diced red onion

1/4 cup shredded cheddar cheese (optional)

1 teaspoon cumin

1/2 teaspoon chili powder

Salt and pepper to taste

Instructions:

Preheat the oven to 375°F (190°C).

In a bowl, combine cooked brown rice, black beans, diced tomatoes, red onion, shredded cheddar cheese (if using), cumin, chili powder, salt, and pepper.

Stuff the bell pepper halves with the rice and bean mixture.

Place stuffed bell peppers on a baking sheet and bake for about 25-30 minutes, until peppers are tender.

Serve warm.

3. Lentil and Vegetable Curry:

Ingredients:

1 cup dried green or brown lentils, rinsed and drained

1 onion, chopped

2 carrots, diced

2 potatoes, diced

1 cup chopped tomatoes

2 cloves garlic, minced

1 tablespoon curry powder

1 teaspoon ground cumin

1/2 teaspoon turmeric

1/4 teaspoon cayenne pepper (adjust to taste)

1 cup vegetable broth

1 cup coconut milk (light or full-fat)

Salt and pepper to taste

Fresh cilantro for garnish

Instructions:

In a large pot, sauté onion, carrots, and potatoes until slightly softened.

Add garlic, curry powder, cumin, turmeric, and cayenne pepper. Cook for another minute.

Add lentils, chopped tomatoes, vegetable broth, and coconut milk.

Bring to a boil, then reduce heat and simmer until lentils and vegetables are tender.

Season with salt and pepper.

Garnish with fresh cilantro before serving.

Serve over cooked brown rice or whole wheat naan.

4. Spinach and Ricotta Stuffed Shells:

Ingredients:

20 jumbo pasta shells, cooked according to package instructions

2 cups fresh spinach, chopped, 1 cup ricotta cheese

1/2 cup shredded mozzarella cheese

1/4 cup grated Parmesan cheese,1 egg

1 clove garlic, minced,1/4 teaspoon nutmeg

Salt and pepper to taste, 2 cups marinara sauce

Instructions:

Preheat the oven to 375°F (190°C).

In a bowl, combine chopped spinach, ricotta cheese, mozzarella cheese, Parmesan cheese, egg, minced garlic, nutmeg, salt, and pepper.

Stuff each cooked pasta shell with the spinach and ricotta mixture.

Spread a thin layer of marinara sauce on the bottom of a baking dish.

Arrange the stuffed shells in the baking dish.

Top with the remaining marinara sauce.

Cover with foil and bake for about 25-30 minutes, until heated through.

Serve warm.

5. *Mediterranean Chickpea Salad:*

Ingredients:

2 cups cooked chickpeas (canned or boiled)

1 cup diced cucumber

1 cup diced tomatoes; 1/2 cup diced red onion

1/2 cup chopped Kalamata olives

1/4 cup crumbled feta cheese

1/4 cup chopped fresh parsley

2 tablespoons lemon juice

2 tablespoons olive oil

1 teaspoon dried oregano

Salt and pepper to taste

Instructions:

In a bowl, combine cooked chickpeas, cucumber, tomatoes, red onion, Kalamata olives, feta cheese, and parsley.

In a separate bowl, whisk lemon juice, olive oil, dried oregano, salt, and pepper.

Drizzle the dressing over the chickpea mixture and toss to combine.

Serve chilled.

6. Veggie Stir-Fried Rice:

Ingredients:

2 cups cooked brown rice

1 cup mixed vegetables (peas, carrots, bell peppers, corn)

1/4 cup diced tofu or tempeh (optional)

2 tablespoons low-sodium soy sauce

1 teaspoon sesame oil, 1/2 teaspoon minced ginger

1 clove garlic, minced, 1/4 cup chopped green onions

1 tablespoon sesame seeds

Instructions:

In a large pan or wok, heat sesame oil over medium-high heat.

Add tofu or tempeh (if using) and cook until golden. Remove from the pan.

In the same pan, sauté mixed vegetables, ginger, and garlic until crisp-tender.

Push the vegetables to the side and add cooked brown rice to the pan.

Stir in cooked tofu or tempeh and pour in soy sauce.

Cook for a few minutes, stirring occasionally.

Garnish with chopped green onions and sesame seeds.

Serve hot.

7. Butternut Squash and Sage Risotto:

Ingredients:

1 cup Arborio rice, 3 cups vegetable broth

2 cups butternut squash, diced

1/4 cup diced onion, 2 cloves garlic, minced

1/4 cup grated Parmesan cheese, 2 tablespoons olive oil

1 tablespoon chopped fresh sage, Salt and pepper to taste

Instructions:

In a pot, heat olive oil over medium heat.

Sauté diced onion until translucent.

Add Arborio rice and minced garlic. Cook for a minute, stirring.

Gradually add vegetable broth, one ladle at a time, stirring constantly until absorbed.

Add diced butternut squash and continue adding broth and stirring.

Once the rice and squash are tender and creamy, remove from heat.

Stir in grated Parmesan cheese and chopped sage.

Season with salt and pepper and Serve warm.

8. *Vegetable and Chickpea Curry:*

Ingredients:

1 cup cooked chickpeas (canned or boiled)

2 cups mixed vegetables (cauliflower, carrots, peas)

1 onion, chopped

2 cloves garlic, minced

1 tablespoon curry powder

1 teaspoon ground cumin

1/2 teaspoon ground coriander

1/4 teaspoon turmeric

1/4 teaspoon cayenne pepper (adjust to taste)

1 cup coconut milk (light or full-fat)

1 cup vegetable broth

1 tablespoon olive oil

Salt and pepper to taste

Fresh cilantro for garnish

Instructions:

In a large pan, heat olive oil over medium heat.

Sauté chopped onion until translucent.

Add minced garlic, curry powder, cumin, coriander, turmeric, and cayenne pepper. Cook for another minute.

Add mixed vegetables and sauté for a few minutes.

Pour in coconut milk and vegetable broth. Bring to a simmer.

Add cooked chickpeas and let the curry simmer until the vegetables are tender.

Season with salt and pepper.

Garnish with fresh cilantro before serving.

Serve over cooked brown rice or whole wheat naan.

9. Cauliflower and Broccoli Alfredo Pasta:

Ingredients:

8 oz whole wheat or gluten-free pasta

2 cups cauliflower florets

1 cup broccoli florets

2 cloves garlic, minced

1/2 cup low-sodium vegetable broth

1/2 cup unsweetened almond milk

1/4 cup grated Parmesan cheese

2 tablespoons nutritional yeast (optional)

1 tablespoon olive oil

1 teaspoon lemon juice

Salt and pepper to taste

Instructions:

Cook pasta according to package instructions. Drain and set aside.

Steam cauliflower and broccoli until tender.

In a blender, combine steamed cauliflower, broccoli, minced garlic, vegetable broth, almond milk, grated Parmesan cheese, nutritional yeast (if using), olive oil, lemon juice, salt, and pepper.

Blend until smooth and creamy.

In a large pot, combine cooked pasta and the cauliflower-broccoli Alfredo sauce.

Heat over low heat, stirring, until warmed through.

Season with additional salt and pepper if needed.

Serve warm.

10. Sweet Potato and Black Bean Tacos:

Ingredients:

8 small corn tortillas

2 cups cooked black beans (canned or boiled)

2 cups roasted sweet potato cubes

1 cup shredded lettuce or cabbage

1/2 cup diced tomatoes

1/4 cup diced red onion

1/4 cup chopped fresh cilantro

1 avocado, sliced

Juice of 1 lime

Salt and pepper to taste

Instructions:

Warm the corn tortillas.

In each tortilla, layer black beans, roasted sweet potato cubes, shredded lettuce or cabbage, diced tomatoes, red onion, chopped cilantro, and avocado slices.

Drizzle with lime juice and season with salt and pepper.

Serve as delicious and nutritious tacos.

11. Eggplant Parmesan:

Ingredients:

1 large eggplant, sliced

1 cup whole wheat breadcrumbs

1/2 cup grated Parmesan cheese

2 eggs, beaten

2 cups marinara sauce

1 cup shredded mozzarella cheese

1 tablespoon olive oil

Fresh basil leaves for garnish

Salt and pepper to taste

Instructions:

Preheat the oven to 375°F (190°C).

Dip eggplant slices in beaten eggs, then coat with breadcrumbs mixed with grated Parmesan cheese.

Heat olive oil in a skillet over medium heat.

Fry eggplant slices until golden on both sides. Drain on paper towels.

In a baking dish, spread a thin layer of marinara sauce.

Layer fried eggplant slices, more marinara sauce, and shredded mozzarella cheese.

Repeat the layers until all ingredients are used, finishing with cheese on top.

Bake for about 20-25 minutes, until cheese is melted and bubbly.

Garnish with fresh basil leaves.

Serve warm over cooked whole wheat pasta or with a side salad.

12. Mushroom and Spinach Frittata:

Ingredients:

6 eggs, 1 cup sliced mushrooms

1 cup chopped spinach; 1/2 cup diced onion

1/4 cup shredded mozzarella cheese

2 tablespoons grated Parmesan cheese, 1 tablespoon olive oil

Salt and pepper to taste

Instructions:

Preheat the oven to 350°F (175°C).

In an oven-safe skillet, heat olive oil over medium heat.

Sauté diced onion and sliced mushrooms until softened.

Add chopped spinach and cook until wilted.

In a bowl, whisk eggs, shredded mozzarella cheese, grated Parmesan cheese, salt, and pepper.

Pour the egg mixture over the sautéed vegetables in the skillet.

Cook on the stovetop for a few minutes until the edges set.

Transfer the skillet to the preheated oven and bake for about 15-20 minutes, until the frittata is cooked through and slightly puffed. Slice and serve warm.

13. Spaghetti Squash Primavera:

Ingredients:

1 medium spaghetti squash

1 cup diced bell peppers (various colors)

1 cup diced zucchini

1 cup diced tomatoes

1/2 cup diced red onion

2 cloves garlic, minced

1/4 cup chopped fresh basil

1/4 cup grated Parmesan cheese

2 tablespoons olive oil

Salt and pepper to taste

Instructions:

Preheat the oven to 375°F (190°C).

Cut the spaghetti squash in half lengthwise and scoop out the seeds.

Brush the inside of the squash halves with olive oil and season with salt and pepper.

Place the squash halves cut-side down on a baking sheet.

Roast in the preheated oven for about 30-40 minutes, until the squash strands are easily separated with a fork.

While the squash is roasting, heat olive oil in a skillet over medium heat.

Sauté diced bell peppers, zucchini, tomatoes, and red onion until softened.

Add minced garlic and cook for another minute.

Once the spaghetti squash is roasted, use a fork to scrape out the strands.

In a bowl, combine the spaghetti squash strands, sautéed vegetables, chopped basil, grated Parmesan cheese, salt, and pepper.

Toss to combine.

Serve warm.

14. Black Bean and Sweet Potato Chili:

Ingredients:

2 cups cooked black beans (canned or boiled)

2 cups diced sweet potatoes

1 cup diced bell peppers (various colors)

1 cup diced tomatoes

1/2 cup diced red onion

2 cloves garlic, minced

2 cups vegetable broth

1 tablespoon chili powder

1 teaspoon ground cumin

1/2 teaspoon smoked paprika

Salt and pepper to taste

Fresh cilantro for garnish

Instructions:

In a large pot, sauté diced sweet potatoes, bell peppers, tomatoes, and red onion until slightly softened.

Add minced garlic, chili powder, cumin, and smoked paprika. Cook for another minute.

Add cooked black beans and vegetable broth.

Bring to a boil, then reduce heat and let the chili simmer until sweet potatoes are tender.

Season with salt and pepper.

Garnish with fresh cilantro before serving.

Serve warm with a side of whole grain bread or brown rice.

15. Mediterranean Stuffed Eggplant:

Ingredients:

2 medium eggplants, 1 cup cooked quinoa

1 cup diced tomatoes, 1/2 cup chopped Kalamata olives

1/4 cup crumbled feta cheese, 1/4 cup chopped fresh parsley

2 tablespoons olive oil, 1 tablespoon balsamic vinegar

1 teaspoon dried oregano

Salt and pepper to taste

Instructions:

Preheat the oven to 375°F (190°C).

Cut the eggplants in half lengthwise and scoop out the flesh, leaving about a 1/2-inch border.

Chop the eggplant flesh and sauté in a pan with olive oil until softened.

In a bowl, combine sautéed eggplant, cooked quinoa, diced tomatoes, Kalamata olives, feta cheese, chopped parsley, balsamic vinegar, dried oregano, salt, and pepper.

Fill the eggplant halves with the quinoa mixture.

Place the stuffed eggplants on a baking sheet and bake for about 25-30 minutes, until the eggplant is tender.

Serve warm.

CHAPTER 6
SNACKING SMARTLY

1. Greek Yogurt Parfait:

1/2 cup plain Greek yogurt

1/4 cup mixed berries (blueberries, raspberries, strawberries)

1 tablespoon chopped nuts (almonds, walnuts)

1 teaspoon honey (optional)

Layer the yogurt, berries, and nuts in a glass. Drizzle with honey if desired.

2. Veggie Sticks with Hummus:

1 cup mixed vegetable sticks (carrots, celery, bell peppers)

2 tablespoons hummus

Dip the veggie sticks into the hummus for a crunchy and satisfying snack.

3. Cottage Cheese and Fruit:

1/2 cup low-fat cottage cheese

1/2 cup diced fresh fruit (such as melon, berries, or pineapple)

Combine cottage cheese and fruit for a protein-packed and refreshing snack.

4. Roasted Chickpeas:

1 cup cooked chickpeas

1 teaspoon olive oil

1/2 teaspoon smoked paprika

1/4 teaspoon cumin

Salt and pepper to taste

Toss chickpeas with olive oil and seasonings, then roast in the oven until crispy.

5. Almond Butter and Apple Slices:

1 medium apple, sliced

1 tablespoon almond butter

Spread almond butter on apple slices for a combination of fiber and healthy fats.

6. Rice Cakes with Avocado:

2 brown rice cakes

1/2 avocado, sliced

Sprinkle of sea salt and black pepper

Top rice cakes with avocado slices and seasonings for a satisfying crunch.

7. Trail Mix:

1/4 cup mixed nuts (almonds, walnuts, cashews)

1/4 cup dried fruits (raisins, cranberries)

1 tablespoon dark chocolate chips (optional)

Create your own trail mix with a variety of nuts, dried fruits, and a touch of dark chocolate.

8. Hard-Boiled Egg:

1 hard-boiled egg

Pinch of salt and pepper

Enjoy a hard-boiled egg for a protein-rich snack with minimal carbs.

9. Edamame:

1 cup steamed edamame (soybeans)

Sprinkle edamame with a bit of sea salt for a protein-packed and satisfying snack.

10. Whole Grain Crackers with Cheese:

6 whole grain crackers

1 oz low-fat cheese

Pair whole grain crackers with a small serving of cheese for a balanced snack.

CHAPTER 6
DESSERTS WITH A HEALTHIER TWIST

1. Berry Parfait:

Ingredients:

1/2 cup mixed berries (blueberries, raspberries, strawberries)

1/2 cup low-fat Greek yogurt

1 tablespoon chopped nuts (almonds, walnuts)

Instructions:

In a glass or bowl, layer mixed berries, Greek yogurt, and chopped nuts.

Repeat the layers if desired.

Serve immediately as a refreshing dessert.

2. Dark Chocolate-Dipped Strawberries:
Ingredients:

6-8 fresh strawberries

1 oz dark chocolate (70% cocoa or higher)

Instructions:

Melt the dark chocolate using a microwave or double boiler.

Dip each strawberry halfway into the melted chocolate.

Place the dipped strawberries on a parchment-lined tray.

Allow the chocolate to cool and set.

Enjoy these delicious treats once the chocolate is firm.

2. Chia Seed Pudding:

Ingredients:

2 tablespoons chia seeds, 1/2 cup unsweetened almond milk

1/2 teaspoon vanilla extract, 1/2 teaspoon cinnamon

Instructions:

In a bowl, mix chia seeds, almond milk, vanilla extract, and cinnamon.

Stir well to ensure the chia seeds are evenly distributed.

Cover the bowl and refrigerate for at least 2 hours or overnight.

Before serving, give the mixture a good stir.

Top with fresh berries or a sprinkle of cinnamon, if desired.

3. Baked Apples with Cinnamon:

Ingredients:

1 medium apple

1/2 teaspoon cinnamon

Instructions:

Preheat the oven to 350°F (175°C).

Core the apple and place it in a baking dish.

Sprinkle cinnamon over the apple.

Bake for about 20-25 minutes, or until the apple is tender.

Enjoy the warm and fragrant baked apple.

4. Yogurt and Fruit Bowl:

Ingredients:

1/2 cup low-fat Greek yogurt

1/2 cup mixed diced fruits (kiwi, mango, berries)

1 tablespoon chopped nuts or seeds

Instructions:

In a bowl, place the Greek yogurt.

Top with diced fruits and chopped nuts or seeds.

Mix gently and enjoy this balanced and satisfying dessert.

5. *Frozen Banana Bites:*

Ingredients:

1 ripe banana, sliced

1 oz dark chocolate (70% cocoa or higher)

Instructions:

Melt the dark chocolate using a microwave or double boiler.

Dip each banana slice halfway into the melted chocolate.

Place the chocolate-dipped banana slices on a parchment-lined tray.

Freeze until the chocolate is firm.

Enjoy these frozen treats straight from the freezer.

6. *Almond Flour Blueberry Muffins:*

Ingredients:

1 cup almond flour, 1/4 cup coconut flour

1/4 teaspoon baking soda, Pinch of salt

2 eggs, 1/4 cup unsweetened almond milk

1/4 cup honey or maple syrup

1/2 cup fresh blueberries

Instructions:

Preheat the oven to 350°F (175°C) and line a muffin tin with paper liners.

In a bowl, whisk together almond flour, coconut flour, baking soda, and salt.

In a separate bowl, beat eggs and mix in almond milk and honey (or maple syrup).

Combine the wet and dry ingredients and gently fold in the blueberries.

Divide the batter evenly among the muffin cups.

Bake for about 20-25 minutes, or until a toothpick inserted into the center of a muffin comes out clean.

Allow the muffins to cool before enjoying.

7. Greek Yogurt and Fruit Popsicles:

Ingredients:

1 cup low-fat Greek yogurt

1/2 cup mixed diced fruits (berries, kiwi, mango)

Instructions:

Blend the Greek yogurt and diced fruits until smooth.

Pour the mixture into popsicle molds.

Insert popsicle sticks and freeze until solid.

Run the molds under warm water to release the popsicles.

Enjoy these refreshing and creamy popsicles.

8. Chocolate Avocado Mousse:

Ingredients:

1 ripe avocado

2 tablespoons unsweetened cocoa powder

2 tablespoons honey or maple syrup

1/2 teaspoon vanilla extract

Instructions:

In a food processor, blend the avocado, cocoa powder, sweetener, and vanilla extract until smooth and creamy.

Taste and adjust sweetness if needed.

Chill the mousse in the refrigerator for at least an hour before serving.

Enjoy this rich and indulgent dessert in moderation.

9. Coconut Rice Pudding:

Ingredients:

1/2 cup brown rice

1 can (13.5 oz) light coconut milk

1/4 teaspoon vanilla extract

1/4 teaspoon ground cinnamon

1 tablespoon chopped nuts (almonds, cashews)

Instructions:

Rinse the brown rice under cold water.

In a pot, combine the rinsed rice and light coconut milk.

Bring to a boil, then reduce the heat to low and cover.

Simmer for about 30-35 minutes, or until the rice is tender and the mixture has thickened.

Stir in the vanilla extract and ground cinnamon.

Divide the rice pudding into serving bowls and sprinkle with chopped nuts.

Serve warm or chilled for a comforting dessert.

CONCLUSION

Congratulations on reaching the end of this transformative journey! This cookbook is your passport to managing pre-diabetes and reversing type-2 diabetes with the power of plant-based nutrition. With 60 delicious recipes and a 30-day meal plan, you're equipped to make positive changes for your health.

By embracing these recipes, you're not just nourishing your body, you're revitalizing your life. Each dish is a step towards better well-being, supported by insights into plant-based nutrition and real-life success stories like Mike's. This cookbook isn't just about food; it's about taking charge of your health and enjoying a life of flavor and vitality.

THANK YOU

Thank you for choosing this "Vegetarian Type-2 Diabetes Diet cookbook". Your commitment to your health and well-being is Inspiring. With each page you're embracing a journey to healthier and tastier life.

Here's to you and your empowered future!

Type-2 Diabetic Daily Meal Planner

Date:

Breakfast	Notes

Lunch	

Dinner	

Snack	Comments

Dessert	

Type-2 Diabetic
Daily Meal Planner

Date:

Breakfast

Notes

Lunch

Dinner

Snack

Comments

Dessert

Type-2 Diabetic
Daily Meal Planner

Date:

Breakfast

Notes

Lunch

Dinner

Snack

Comments

Dessert

Type-2 Diabetic
Daily Meal Planner

Date:

Breakfast

Notes

Lunch

Dinner

Snack

Comments

Dessert

Type-2 Diabetic
Daily Meal Planner

Date:

Breakfast

Notes

Lunch

Dinner

Snack

Comments

Dessert

Type-2 Diabetic
Daily Meal Planner

Date:

Breakfast

Notes

Lunch

Dinner

Snack

Comments

Dessert

Type-2 Diabetic
Daily Meal Planner

Date:

Breakfast	Notes
Lunch	
Dinner	
Snack	**Comments**
Dessert	

Type-2 Diabetic
Daily Meal Planner

Date:

Breakfast

Notes

Lunch

Dinner

Snack

Comments

Dessert

Type-2 Diabetic
Daily Meal Planner

Date:

Breakfast

Notes

Lunch

Dinner

Snack

Comments

Dessert

Type-2 Diabetic
Daily Meal Planner

Date:

Breakfast

Notes

Lunch

Dinner

Snack

Comments

Dessert

Type-2 Diabetic
Daily Meal Planner

Date:

Breakfast

Notes

Lunch

Dinner

Snack

Comments

Dessert

Type-2 Diabetic
Daily Meal Planner

Date:

Breakfast

Notes

Lunch

Dinner

Snack

Comments

Dessert

Type-2 Diabetic
Daily Meal Planner

Date:

| Breakfast | Notes |

| Lunch |

| Dinner |

| Snack | Comments |

| Dessert |

Type-2 Diabetic
Daily Meal Planner

Date:

Breakfast		Notes

Lunch	

Dinner	

Snack		Comments

Dessert	

Type-2 Diabetic
Daily Meal Planner

Date:

Breakfast

Notes

Lunch

Dinner

Snack

Comments

Dessert

Type-2 Diabetic
Daily Meal Planner

Date:

Breakfast

Notes

Lunch

Dinner

Snack

Comments

Dessert

Type-2 Diabetic
Daily Meal Planner

Date:

Breakfast

Lunch

Dinner

Snack

Dessert

Notes

Comments

Type-2 Diabetic
Daily Meal Planner

Date:

Breakfast

Notes

Lunch

Dinner

Snack

Comments

Dessert

Type-2 Diabetic
Daily Meal Planner

Date:

Breakfast	Notes

Lunch

Dinner

Snack	Comments

Dessert

Type-2 Diabetic
Daily Meal Planner

Date:

Breakfast	Notes

Lunch

Dinner

Snack

Comments

Dessert

Type-2 Diabetic
Daily Meal Planner

Date:

Breakfast

Notes

Lunch

Dinner

Snack

Comments

Dessert

Type-2 Diabetic
Daily Meal Planner   Date:

Breakfast

Notes

Lunch

Dinner

Snack

Comments

Dessert

Type-2 Diabetic
Daily Meal Planner

Date:

Breakfast	Notes

Lunch

Dinner

Snack	Comments

Dessert

Type-2 Diabetic
Daily Meal Planner

Date:

Breakfast

Notes

Lunch

Dinner

Snack

Comments

Dessert

Type-2 Diabetic
Daily Meal Planner

Date:

Breakfast

Lunch

Dinner

Snack

Dessert

Notes

Comments

Type-2 Diabetic
Daily Meal Planner

Date:

Breakfast	Notes

Lunch

Dinner

Snack

Comments

Dessert

Type-2 Diabetic
Daily Meal Planner

Date:

Breakfast	Notes

Lunch	

Dinner	

Snack	Comments

Dessert	

Type-2 Diabetic
Daily Meal Planner

Date:

Breakfast

Notes

Lunch

Dinner

Snack

Comments

Dessert

Type-2 Diabetic
Daily Meal Planner

Date:

Breakfast

Notes

Lunch

Dinner

Snack

Comments

Dessert

Type-2 Diabetic
Daily Meal Planner

Date:

Breakfast

Notes

Lunch

Dinner

Snack

Comments

Dessert

THANK YOU

Thank you for choosing the "Vegetarian Type 2 Diabetic Diet Cookbook." Your commitment to health and well-being is inspiring. With each page, you're embracing a journey to a healthier, tastier life. Here's to you and your empowered future!

Printed in Great Britain
by Amazon

49793125R00066